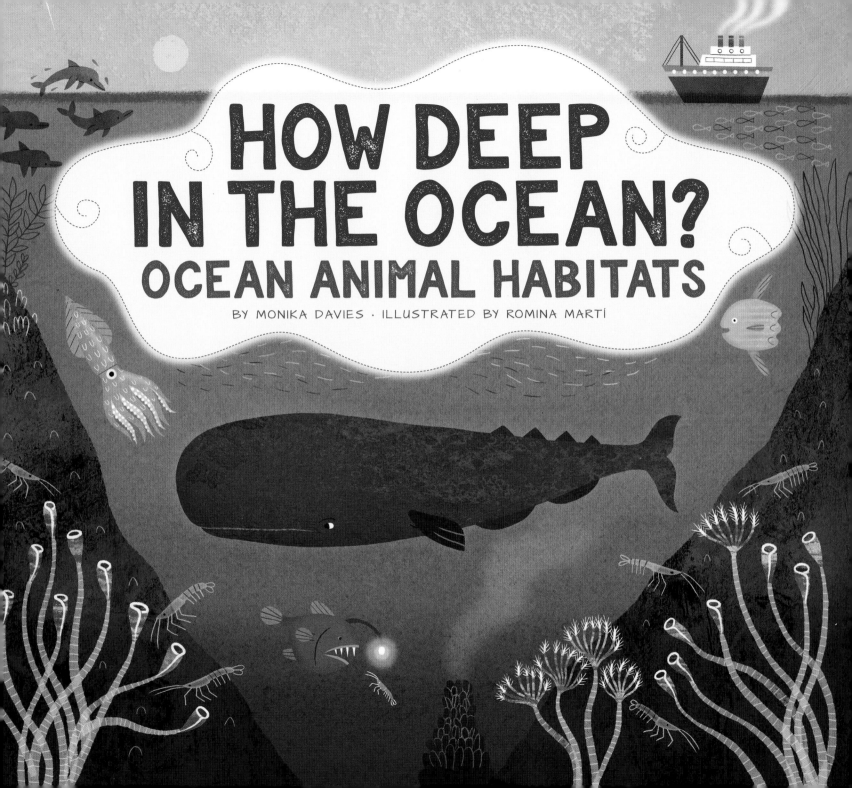

HOW DEEP IN THE OCEAN?
OCEAN ANIMAL HABITATS

BY MONIKA DAVIES · ILLUSTRATED BY ROMINA MARTÍ

Amicus Illustrated and Amicus Ink
are published by Amicus
P.O. Box 1329
Mankato, MN 56002
www.amicuspublishing.us

Library of Congress Cataloging-in-Publication Data
Names: Davies, Monika, author. | Marti, Romina, illustrator.
Title: How deep in the ocean? : ocean animal habitats / by Monika
    Davies ; Illustrated by Romina Marti.
Other titles: Ocean animal habitats
Description: Mankato, MN : Amicus Illustrated, [2019] | Series:
    Animals measure up | Audience: K to grade 3. | Includes
    bibliographical references and index.
Identifiers: LCCN 2017057753 (print) | LCCN 2017058962
    (ebook) | ISBN 9781681514666 (pdf) | ISBN 9781681513843
    (library binding) | ISBN 9781681523040 (pbk.)
Subjects: LCSH: Marine animals—Juvenile literature. |
    Oceanography—Juvenile literature. | Pacific Ocean—Juvenile
    literature.
Classification: LCC QL122.2 (ebook) | LCC QL122.2 .D3785 2019
    (print) | DDC 578.77—dc23
LC record available at https://lccn.loc.gov/2017057753

Editor: Rebecca Glaser
Designer: Kathleen Petelinsek

Printed in the United States of America

HC 10 9 8 7 6 5 4 3 2 1
PB 10 9 8 7 6 5 4 3 2 1

About the Author

Living on the west coast of Canada, Monika Davies likes
to dip her toes in the Pacific Ocean. One day, she hopes
to dive through the sunlight zone to meet new ocean
friends. Monika graduated from the University of British
Columbia with a bachelor of fine arts in creative writing.
She has written over eighteen books for young readers.

About the Illustrator

Romina Martí is an illustrator who lives and works in
Barcelona, Spain, where her ideas come to life for all
audiences. She loves to discover and draw all kinds of
creatures from around the planet, who then become the
main characters for the majority of her work. To learn
more, go to: rominamarti.com.

Say hello to the Pacific Ocean! This is the world's deepest "bucket" of water. Have you ever wondered how deep ocean animals swim? Let's find out!

Layer by layer, this ocean hides treasures. At the top is the brightest ocean layer, the sunlight zone. Here, the beams of a smiling sun warm the water.

SUNLIGHT ZONE

0 FEET
10
20
30
40
50
60
70
80
90
100
110
120
130
140
150

METERS 0

5

10

15

20

SUNLIGHT ZONE

25

30

35

40

45

Near the shore, sea plants sprout in shades of green. Some plants, like tiny phytoplankton, float all across the ocean. For many marine animals, this is home.

A green sea turtle soars past. They like to bask in the warmth of the sunlight zone. Here, sea turtles can find beds of seagrass in shallow waters. This is one of their favorite foods. The lush green blades need light to grow.

SUNLIGHT ZONE

SUNLIGHT ZONE

SUNLIGHT ZONE

FT
10
50
100
150
200
250
300
350
400
450
500
550
600

We travel down, deeper into the sunlight zone. It's 305 feet (93 m) back to the top. Imagine the Statue of Liberty went swimming. This is how far she could reach!

A blue whale surges past. These whales live on a big diet of krill. They have huge stomachs. They must dive deep to find enough to eat.

SUNLIGHT ZONE

0 M
50
100
150
200

500
FT

1,000

1,500

2,000

2,500

3,000

3,500

150
M

300

450

600

750

900

1,050

TWILIGHT ZONE

TWILIGHT ZONE

10

Deeper still, you go. It's a steep drop to the next layer. This is the twilight zone. Here, the water grows cold. The sun only blinks through the waves. Plants cannot grow. Animals must find ways to survive in this darkness.

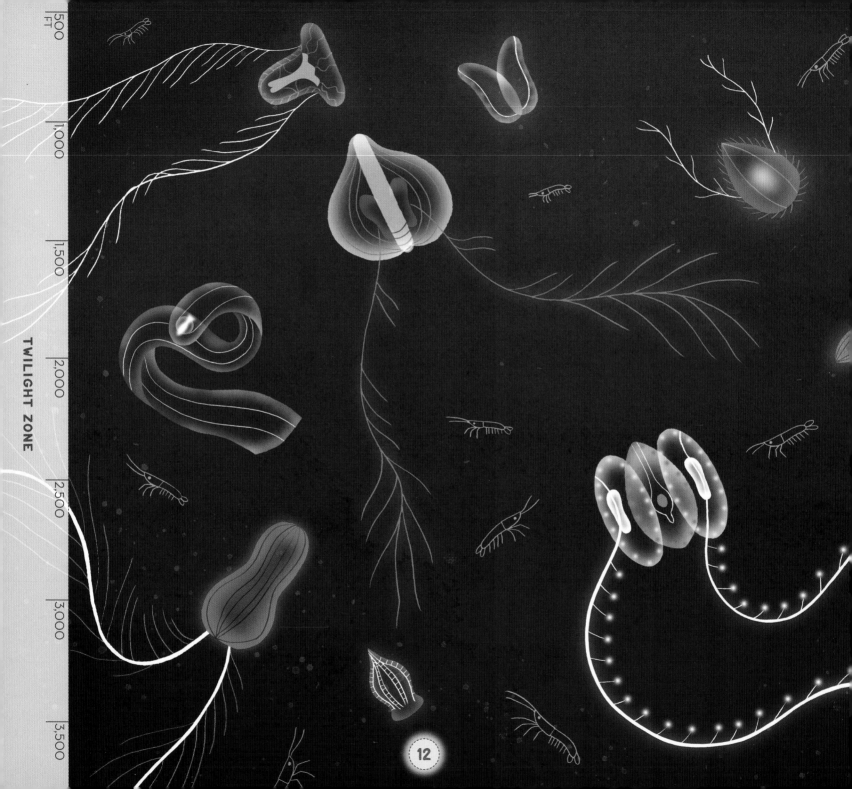

1,000

1,500

TWILIGHT ZONE

2,000

2,500

3,000

3,500

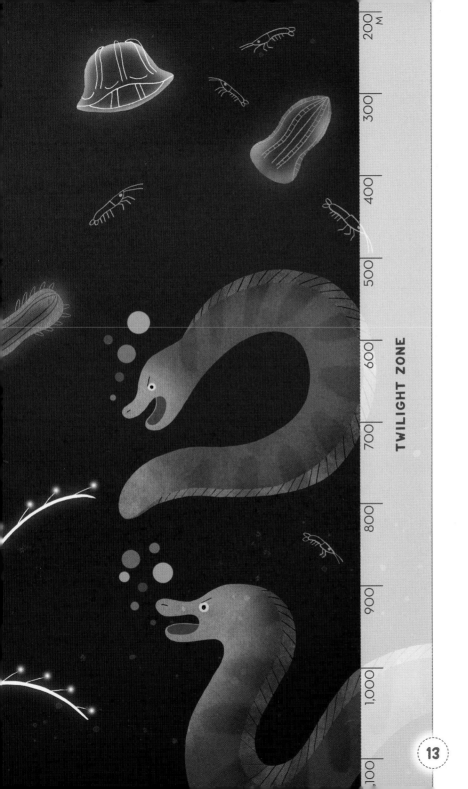

200 M

300

400

500

TWILIGHT ZONE

600

700

800

900

1,000

1,100

Comb jellies bob in and out. Some are transparent. Others are red. They are hard to spot in the deep sea. Sometimes, comb jellies light up. **Flash!** Some think this is to scare off predators.

Deep-sea hatchetfish swing by. These small, silvery fish are flat like a sideways pancake. Their round eyes help them see in the dark. These fish can live 3,000 feet (914 m) underwater. You would need to climb down two Willis Towers to reach that far!

0 FT

500

1,000

1,500

2,000

2,500

3,000

3,500

4,000

4,500

TWILIGHT ZONE

0 M

100

200

300

400

500

600

700

800

900

1,000

1,100

1,200

TWILIGHT ZONE

15

As you sink lower, every ray of sun is gone. The water is a cold, inky black. This is the ocean's midnight zone. There are no crowds here.

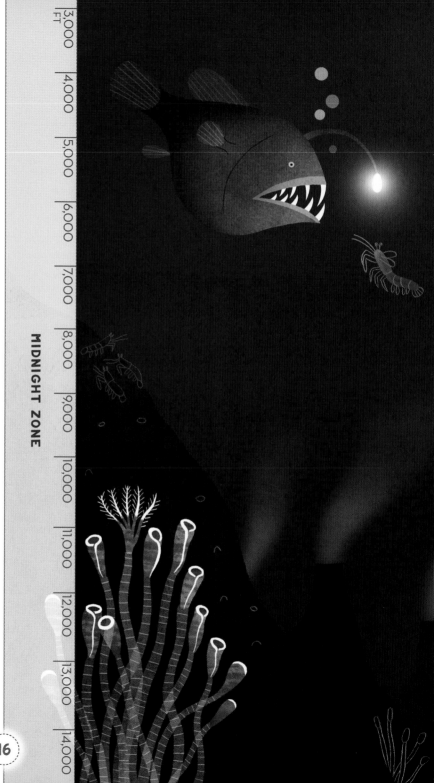

MIDNIGHT ZONE

3,000 FT

4,000

5,000

6,000

7,000

8,000

9,000

10,000

11,000

12,000

13,000

14,000

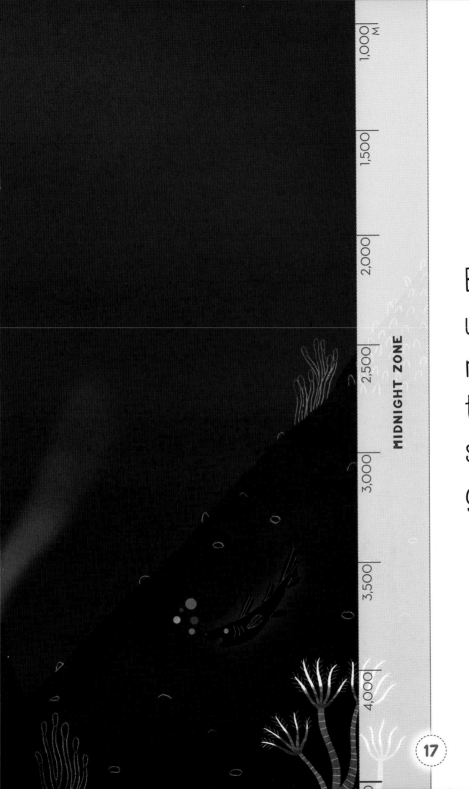

1,000 M

1,500

2,000

2,500

MIDNIGHT ZONE

3,000

3,500

4,000

But some fish light up this dark water. Anglerfish have a "fishing rod" on their head. The end of the rod shines light to draw in shrimp. Then, snap! The anglerfish gobbles them up.

3,000
FT

4,000

5,000

6,000

7,000

8,000

9,000

10,000

11,000

12,000

13,000

14,000

1,000
M

1,500

2,000

2,500

3,000

3,500

4,000

The black swallower is always on the prowl for food. Sometimes, it must wait a long time for its next meal. The black swallower has a stretchy stomach. It can eat fish twice its size! This way, it stays full for a long time.

SUNLIGHT ZONE

TWILIGHT ZONE

MIDNIGHT ZONE

ABYSS

TRENCHES

0 FT

5,000

10,000

15,000

20,000

25,000

30,000

35,000

Below the midnight zone lies the abyss. Only a few sea cucumbers and other animals live this deep. The ocean floor dips and dives into deep trenches.

Challenger Deep marks the deepest trench—the very bottom of the Pacific Ocean. It is 36,070 feet (11,000 meters) down. That's longer than a climb to the top of Mount Everest! There is still so much to explore.

SUNLIGHT ZONE
TWILIGHT ZONE
MIDNIGHT ZONE
ABYSS
TRENCHES

0 M
2,500
5,000
7,500
10,000

LAYERS OF THE OCEAN

**SUNLIGHT
ZONE**

660 FT (200 M)

**TWILIGHT
ZONE**

3,300 FT (1000 M)

**MIDNIGHT
ZONE**

13,100 FT (4,000 M)

ABYSS

19,700 FT (6,000 M)

TRENCHES

36,070 FT (11,000 M)
CHALLENGER DEEP

GLOSSARY

abyss The ocean layer near the ocean floor, from 13,100 feet (4,000 m) to 19,700 feet (6,000m).

krill Very small creatures in the ocean that are the main food of some whales.

marine Of or relating to the sea or the plants and animals that live in the sea.

midnight zone Third layer of the ocean, from 3,300 feet (1,000 m) to 13,100 feet (4,000 m) underwater.

predator An animal that hunts and eats other animals.

sunlight zone First layer of the ocean, which is from the ocean's surface to 660 feet (200 m) underwater.

transparent Able to be seen through.

trench A long, narrow ditch in the ocean floor.

twilight zone Second layer of the ocean, which is from 660 feet (200 m) to 3,300 feet (1,000 m) underwater.

READ MORE

Boothroyd, Jennifer. **Let's Visit the Ocean**. Minneapolis: Lerner Publications, 2017.

Lynch, Seth. **There's an Ocean in my Backyard!** New York: Gareth Stevens Publishing, 2017.

Oachs, Emily Rose. **Pacific Ocean**. Minneapolis: Bellwether Media, 2016.

WEBSITES

How Tiny Are You Compared To the Biggest Sea Creatures? – Discovery Kids

http://discoverykids.com/videos/how-tiny-are-you-compared-to-the-biggest-sea-creatures/

See how you stack up size-wise compared to the largest sea creatures in the world.

Ocean Portal – National Geographic Kids

http://kids.nationalgeographic.com/explore/ocean-portal/

Dive deep into the ocean with National Geographic for sea creature profiles, games, and more!

Under the Sea Animals - Easy Science for Kids

http://easyscienceforkids.com/animals/under-the-sea-animals/

Learn about horseshoe crabs, jawless fish, sea mollusks, and more!

Every effort has been made to ensure that these websites are appropriate for children. However, because of the nature of the Internet, it is impossible to guarantee that these sites will remain active indefinitely or that their contents will not be altered.